WHISPERS OF A WEARY MIND
ECHOES OF THOUGHTS, DREAMS, AND SILENT STRUGGLES

JASNEET SINGH

BLUEROSE PUBLISHERS
India | U.K.

Copyright © Jasneet Singh 2025

All rights reserved by author. No part of this publication may be reproduced, stored in a retrieval system or transmitted in any form or by any means, electronic, mechanical, photocopying, recording or otherwise, without the prior permission of the author. Although every precaution has been taken to verify the accuracy of the information contained herein, the publisher assume no responsibility for any errors or omissions. No liability is assumed for damages that may result from the use of information contained within.

BlueRose Publishers takes no responsibility for any damages, losses, or liabilities that may arise from the use or misuse of the information, products, or services provided in this publication.

For permissions requests or inquiries regarding this publication, please contact:

BLUEROSE PUBLISHERS
www.BlueRoseONE.com
info@bluerosepublishers.com
+91 8882 898 898
+4407342408967

ISBN: 978-93-7018-858-7

Cover design: Daksh
Typesetting: Tanya Raj Upadhyay

First Edition: April 2025

Table of Contents

Chapter 1: The Weight of Thoughts 1

Chapter 2: The Breaking Point 7

Chapter 3: The Weight of Expectations 15

Chapter 4: A New Dawn 23

Chapter 5: Shadows of Doubt 30

Chapter G: A Flicker of Hope 36

Chapter 1:
The Weight of Thoughts

The sun had barely started its ascent when Reena stirred from her restless sleep. The thin veil of dawn crept through the curtains, casting soft shadows across the room. She lay in bed, staring at the ceiling, her mind racing with a cacophony of thoughts. It was a familiar struggle—her mind was a battleground, and today, like many days before, the negative thoughts seemed to be winning.

"Another day, another fight," she muttered under her breath, her voice barely a whisper, as if the very act of speaking would summon the weight of her worries into the room. Reena turned to her side, glancing at Raman, her husband, who lay sound asleep next to her. A small sigh escaped her lips as she marveled at his stillness. Unlike her, he seemed to carry a certain peace, even in the depths of their shared struggles.

Raman had been trying to make ends meet with odd jobs ever since his last full-time position fell through. He was a man of resilience, but the uncertainty of their financial situation loomed over

Reena like a dark cloud. She felt a pang of guilt for feeling burdened when he bore the weight of their expenses and responsibilities with such grace. But guilt was a familiar visitor, often knocking at her door uninvited.

As she slipped out of bed, careful not to wake him, Reena made her way to the small kitchen. The scent of the previous night's dinner still lingered in the air, a reminder of their modest means. She turned on the kettle, the whistle soon filling the silence, and

began to prepare breakfast. Each motion was mechanical, almost robotic, as her mind continued to spiral into a whirlpool of negativity.

"What if Raman doesn't find work today? What if Aman doesn't get into a good school? What if we lose everything?" The questions invaded her thoughts like uninvited guests, each one more suffocating than the last. She tried to shake them off, reminding herself that her worries rarely materialized. But reason often fell short when faced with anxiety.

Aman, their seven-year-old son, bounded into the kitchen, his energy a stark contrast to her heavy heart. He was the light in her life, a small beacon of hope that made the struggles bearable. "Good morning, Mom!" he chirped, his eyes sparkling with the innocence of youth.

"Good morning, Aman," Reena replied, forcing a smile that felt foreign on her lips. She poured him a bowl of cereal, the familiar routine providing a semblance of normalcy in her chaotic mind.

As he munched on his breakfast, Aman began to chatter about his plans for the day. "We're learning about space in school! Did you know that astronauts float in space? I want to be an astronaut, Mom!" His excitement was contagious, and for a moment, Reena felt a flicker of joy.

"Space is amazing, isn't it?" she said, her tone brightening. "You'll have to tell me all about it when you get home."

"Promise!" Aman replied, his mouth full of cereal, causing Reena to chuckle softly. But just as quickly, the weight returned. What if she couldn't provide him with the opportunities he deserved? The thought gnawed at her insides.

After breakfast, Raman emerged from the bedroom, his face slightly creased with sleep. He offered her a warm smile, which she returned half-heartedly. "What's on the agenda today?" he asked, pouring himself a cup of coffee.

"I thought I'd clean the house and maybe start on that new recipe I found," she replied, trying to sound upbeat.

"Sounds good. I'll be heading out shortly to look for some work," he said, his tone casual. Reena nodded, but inside, a wave of anxiety washed over her. What if he didn't find anything? What if they had to make cuts again? The previous month had already been tight, and she feared the future like a specter lurking just out of sight.

As Raman left, Reena felt the house swallow her whole. The silence was deafening, a stark contrast to the chaos in her mind. She moved through the rooms, picking up toys, dusting surfaces, but her thoughts were relentless, like a storm that wouldn't pass.

"Why is it so hard?" she whispered to herself, her voice echoing in the empty living room. "Why can't I just breathe? Why can't I just trust that everything will be okay?"

In her heart, Reena had always been a spiritual person. She found solace in her faith, a connection to something greater than herself. Yet, lately, that connection felt frayed. She often found herself questioning the very essence of her beliefs. "If God is good, why is life so hard?" The question haunted her, and she often found herself in silent conversations with the divine, pleading for answers that never came.

That afternoon, as she sat on the worn-out sofa, staring at the wall, the frustration bubbled over. "What do you want from me?" she shouted, her voice breaking the silence, startling even herself. It was a question directed at the universe, at God, at everything she believed in. "Why do you let us suffer? Why do you let my husband struggle? Why do you let my thoughts consume me?"

The words hung in the air, heavy and accusatory. For a moment, Reena felt a release, as if voicing her anger had lifted a weight from her chest. But the relief was fleeting, soon replaced by a gnawing guilt for questioning her faith. "What kind of believer am I?" she thought, her heart heavy with shame.

That evening, when Raman returned, he wore a weary smile, and his eyes carried the weight of the day. "I spoke to a few people. I think I might have a lead on a part-time job," he said, hope flickering in his voice.

"Really?" Reena replied, her heart lifting slightly. "That's great news!" But the joy was tinged with anxiety. What if it fell through? What if it wasn't enough?

As they sat together, sharing a simple dinner, Aman animatedly recounted his day at school. "We saw videos of astronauts floating in space! I want to be one!" he exclaimed, his enthusiasm infectious.

Raman and Reena exchanged a glance, a silent understanding passing between them. They both wanted to give Aman the world, to nurture his dreams.

But the weight of their own realities pressed down on them like a heavy shroud.

Later that night, as Reena lay in bed next to Raman, she felt the familiar pull of her negative thoughts. "What if we can't afford to send Aman to college? What if we fail him?" The questions spiraled in her mind, relentless and unforgiving.

"Reena?" Raman's voice broke through her thoughts. "Are you okay?"

She turned to him, forcing a smile. "Just tired," she lied.

"Don't worry so much. We'll figure it out," he said, placing a comforting hand on her shoulder.

His reassurance was a balm, but it did little to quiet the storm inside her. As she closed her eyes, she whispered a prayer, not for answers, but for peace. The weight of her thoughts felt heavier than ever, a burden she wasn't sure she could carry. The night stretched on, and Reena lay awake, wrestling with her fears, her hopes, and the relentless voice in her mind.

Chapter 2:
The Breaking Point

The morning sun spilled through the curtains, illuminating the small kitchen with a warm glow, but Reena felt far from warm inside. She stood by the sink, staring blankly at the dishes piled high, the remnants of last night's dinner still clinging to the plates. Each dish felt like a weight, a reminder of the responsibilities that loomed over her like dark clouds threatening to unleash a storm. The once-familiar sound of water running felt foreign, a stark contrast to the tempest swirling in her mind.

"Mom, can I have cereal again?" Aman's voice broke through her reverie, his small figure peeking around the corner. He was clad in his pajamas, his hair tousled and wild from sleep. The innocence in his eyes tugged at her heart, but the familiar pang of guilt washed over her. She couldn't even muster the energy to make him a proper breakfast.

"Sure, sweetheart," she replied, forcing a smile that felt more like a mask than a genuine expression. As she poured the cereal and milk, her mind drifted into the abyss of worries that had become her constant companions.

"What if we can't pay the rent this month? What if the landlord comes by? What if I can't give Aman the life he deserves?" The questions tumbled through her thoughts like a relentless waterfall, each one more suffocating than the last. She felt trapped in a cycle of negativity, her spirit weighed down by the gravity of her circumstances.

Raman had been searching for work tirelessly, but each rejection letter felt like a dagger, piercing through the fragile hope they had clung to. The once vibrant dreams they had shared seemed to wither away, replaced by the harsh reality of their financial struggles. Reena's heart ached for him; he was a man of integrity and hard work, yet the world seemed determined to keep him at bay.

As she watched Aman munching on his cereal, she felt a flicker of warmth in her heart, a reminder of what mattered most. But the flicker was quickly extinguished by the impending dread of their situation. The rent was overdue, and the landlord had been unusually patient, but patience had its limits. Reena's mind spiraled into dark corners, wondering what would happen if they lost their home. Where would they go? How would they start over?

Just as she was lost in her thoughts, the doorbell rang, slicing through the stillness of the morning. Reena's heart raced, fear gripping her. It was too early for visitors. She glanced at Aman, who was obliviously focused on his cereal, and then back at the door. Taking a deep breath, she wiped her hands on a dish towel and made her way to the door, her heart pounding in her chest.

When she opened it, the sight of their landlord greeted her—Mr. Kumar, a gruff man with a no-nonsense demeanor. The moment she saw his serious expression, a chill ran down her spine.

"Reena," he said, his voice low but firm. "We need to talk."

Her stomach dropped. "Is it about the rent?" she asked, her voice barely above a whisper.

He nodded, stepping inside without waiting for an invitation. "I've been patient, but it's been two months now. You need to pay up or we'll have to discuss your options."

Reena felt her heart race. The walls seemed to close in on her, the air thick with fear and shame. "Please, Mr. Kumar, we're doing everything we can. My husband is looking for work, and—"

"I understand, but I can't keep waiting indefinitely," he interrupted, his tone resolute. "I'll give you until the end of the week. After that, I'll have no choice but to start eviction proceedings."

His words hung in the air like a dark cloud, and Reena felt herself choke on the weight of them. "Thank you," she managed to say, even as her heart shattered into a million pieces. The reality of their situation crashed down around her, the walls of their home feeling less like a sanctuary and more like a prison.

After Mr. Kumar left, Reena leaned against the door, the cold wood pressing against her back as she tried to steady her breathing. She could hear Aman's cheerful chatter in the background, but it felt like a distant echo, a world away from her turmoil.

"Mom, who was that?" Aman asked, his voice filled with innocent curiosity.

"Just the landlord, sweetie," she replied, forcing another smile, though it felt like a betrayal to her own feelings. "Everything's fine."

But everything was not fine. As she returned to the kitchen, the weight of despair settled heavily on her shoulders. She felt like she was drowning in a sea of anxiety, each wave threatening to pull her under.

"Why is this happening?" she whispered to herself, her voice trembling with frustration. "Why can't we catch a break?"

Her thoughts spiraled further into darkness. "What kind of mother am I? I can't even provide a stable home for my son. I'm failing him, failing Raman." The guilt twisted like a knife in her gut, and she felt a surge of anger directed not only at her circumstances but also at herself.

"God, why do you let this happen?" she shouted, her voice breaking. "I've always believed in you, but where are you now? Why aren't you helping us?"

Her words echoed in the empty kitchen, a raw and desperate plea that hung in the air. She had always found solace in her faith, but now it felt like a cruel joke. How could she trust in a higher power when everything around her was crumbling?

Aman's laughter suddenly broke through her despair, pulling her back from the brink. She turned to see him playing with his toys, completely unaware of the storm raging within her. The sight of his innocent joy sparked a flicker of something deep within her—a reminder of what was truly important.

But just as quickly, the flicker was snuffed out by the looming reality of their situation. Her brother Vikram's voice echoed in her mind, taunting her with every failure, every struggle. "You'll never amount to anything. Look at you, living in a rundown apartment, with a husband who can't keep a job. How pathetic."

The words stung, and Reena felt anger rise in her chest. Vikram had always been the successful sibling, the one who never missed an opportunity to remind her of her shortcomings. She had always tried to brush off his taunts, but now they felt like daggers, piercing through her already fragile spirit.

"Why do I let him get to me?" she thought. "Why do I care what he thinks?"

But the truth was, she did care. She cared because she had always wanted to prove herself, to show him that she was more than just a housewife, more than someone who struggled to make ends meet. But with every setback, every moment of despair, it felt like she was losing that battle.

That evening, when Raman returned home, his face was drawn, and his eyes carried the weight of the world. "I went to a few places today, but nothing panned out," he said, his voice tinged with disappointment.

Reena felt her heart sink. "Raman, I—"

But before she could finish, he continued, "It's okay. I'll keep trying. We'll figure it out."

His optimism was admirable, but it only deepened her sense of helplessness. She wanted to be strong for him, to be the pillar he could lean on, but all she felt was a growing chasm of despair between them.

"Raman, the landlord came by today," she said, her voice trembling. "He gave us until the end of the week to pay the rent or we'll be evicted."

His expression shifted, the weight of her words settling heavily on his shoulders. "What? Reena, why didn't you tell me sooner?"

"I didn't want to worry you," she replied, tears threatening to spill.

"Worry me? We need to face this together," he said, frustration creeping into his tone.

"I know," she whispered, feeling the familiar guilt wash over her. "I'm sorry, I just—"

But the words caught in her throat as the emotions surged. The weight of their struggles felt insurmountable, and for a moment, she felt as if she was on the brink of breaking.

"Reena, we'll find a way. We always do," Raman said, reaching out to take her hand.

But even his reassurance felt like a temporary balm on a wound that ran too deep. She wanted to believe him, to cling to the hope that they would find a way out, but the darkness loomed large, whispering doubts into her ear.

As they sat together in silence, Aman's laughter echoed in the background, a stark reminder of the innocence they were fighting to protect. Reena closed her eyes, trying to find a flicker of hope amidst the darkness, but the weight of her fears pressed down on her like an anchor, and she felt herself sinking further into despair.

In that moment, as the night stretched on and the shadows deepened, Reena realized she was at a breaking point. The storm inside her had grown too fierce to ignore, and she could no longer pretend that everything was okay. The walls of her faith felt like they were crumbling, and she was left standing amidst the rubble, searching for a way to rebuild.

Chapter 3:
The Weight of Expectations

The sun dipped low in the sky, casting long shadows across the room, as Reena sat on the edge of the bed, cradling her head in her hands. The oppressive silence was only broken by the distant sound of Aman's laughter as he played with his toys in the living room. But even that cheerfulness felt like a distant echo, unable to penetrate the heavy fog of despair that had settled over her.

Raman entered the room, his expression a mix of determination

and weariness. "Reena, I've been thinking..." he began, his voice steady but tinged with the weight of their current struggles. "Maybe we should ask Vikram for help."

Reena lifted her head slowly, her heart sinking at the mention of her brother's name. Vikram had always been the golden child, the one who seemingly had everything handed to him on a silver platter. The thought of reaching out to him sent waves of anxiety crashing over her. "Raman, I don't know if that's a good idea," she replied, her voice barely above a whisper.

"Look," he said, taking a step closer, "we're in a tight spot. We need money to pay the rent, and I can't think of anyone else who could help us right now. Just a temporary loan until I find work."

Reena's mind raced with memories of Vikram's sharp tongue and biting comments. The last time she had spoken to him, he had taken great pleasure in reminding her of every misstep she had ever made. "He won't help us, Raman. He'll just use it against us," she said, shaking her head as a knot of dread tightened in her stomach.

"I'll only ask for twenty-five thousand rupees. It's not a lot, but it could buy us some time," Raman insisted, his voice firm but gentle.

Reena's heart ached at the thought of Raman humbling himself before Vikram, who had always looked down on her family and their struggles. "But what if he refuses? What if he makes it worse?"

"Then we'll figure something out," he replied, his eyes locked onto hers with a fierce determination. "We've fought through so much already. I just need you to trust me on this one."

With a heavy sigh, Reena nodded, though her stomach twisted in knots at the prospect. "Okay, but I can't bear to see you humiliated by him."

Raman reached out, taking her hands in his. "I promise you, I won't let him get to me. We need this for Aman. We have to try."

As the evening wore on, the air in their small apartment felt thick with tension. Reena could hardly focus on anything but the impending conversation between Raman and Vikram. When the moment finally arrived, she watched from the kitchen as Raman picked up the phone, his face set in determination, and dialed her brother's number.

With each ring, Reena felt her heart race, a mix of anxiety and dread coursing through her veins. Then, she heard Vikram's voice on the other end, sharp and commanding. "What do you want?" he barked, a tone of irritation lacing his words.

"Vikram, it's me, Raman," her husband replied, his voice steady despite the tension hanging in the air. "I need to ask you for a favor."

Reena held her breath, straining to hear every word as she washed the dishes, pretending to be busy. "What kind of favor?"

Vikram's voice dripped with skepticism.

"We're in a tough spot right now, and I was wondering if you could lend us twenty-five thousand rupees. Just until I get back on my feet," Raman explained, his words measured and calm.

"Money?" Vikram scoffed. "Is that what you're calling me for? To beg for money like a charity case?"

Reena's heart sank, and she felt the urge to step in and defend Raman, but she knew better than to interrupt. She could hear the disdain in Vikram's tone, and it made her stomach churn.

"Vikram, please, this isn't easy for me," Raman said, his voice strained but resolute. "We're trying to keep our home. I wouldn't ask if it weren't important."

There was a long pause, and Reena could only imagine the contemptuous look on Vikram's face as he processed Raman's request. "You really think I'd give you money after everything? You're a failure, Raman. You can't even take care of your own family. How pathetic," Vikram spat, and Reena felt the words cut into her like a blade.

Raman's silence spoke volumes, and Reena felt a mix of anger and hurt for him. How could Vikram be so cruel? "Just a little help," she whispered to herself, tears welling in her eyes. "Can't he see how hard we're trying?"

"Don't even think about it, Raman. You've made your bed, now lie

in it," Vikram continued, his voice dripping with malice. "You're nothing without my help, and you know it. Good luck finding someone else to support your pathetic life."

The call ended abruptly, and Reena felt her heart shatter into a million pieces. She turned to see Raman staring blankly at the phone, his expression one of defeat. "I'm sorry," she said softly, stepping closer to him.

Raman shook his head, his eyes clouded with frustration and hurt. "I knew he wouldn't help, but hearing him say those things... it's just so degrading."

Reena reached out to comfort him, but her own emotions were bubbling beneath the surface. "He's a coward, Raman. You're not pathetic. You're fighting for us, for our family."

"But it doesn't feel that way," he said, his voice cracking. "I feel like I'm failing you both. I can't even provide for my family."

Reena's heart ached at the sight of his vulnerability. She wanted to tell him that they would get through this together, but the shadows of self-doubt loomed large in her mind.

Suddenly, the phone rang again, and Reena's heart leaped into her throat. She could feel the tension in the air as Raman answered it again, a hint of apprehension in his voice. "Hello?"

It was Vikram again, and this time Reena could hear the condescension in his tone even from across the room. "I just

wanted to remind you that you're a burden. I'd be careful about how you treat that burden, or it might just crush you," he taunted.

"Vikram, that's enough," Raman said firmly, though the hurt was evident in his voice.

"No, it's not enough. You need to hear this. You're a failure, and you always will be. You think I'm going to bail you out? Let me be clear: you're on your own. And if you want to keep your pride, stop asking me for help."

Vikram's words echoed in the small apartment, suffocating the air with their venom. Reena felt herself shaking, her heart pounding as she listened to the insults fly.

"Why do you even bother with this loser, Reena?" Vikram continued, his voice dripping with disdain. "You could have had a real life, but look at you—stuck in a dead-end marriage with someone who can't even keep a job."

Tears streamed down Reena's face as she listened to her brother tear apart everything she held dear. "Please, stop," she begged, her voice breaking. "He's trying his best."

"His best isn't good enough. You know it, and deep down, he knows it too," Vikram shot back. "You two deserve each other. Take your pathetic life and make the best of it, because no one else will."

When the call ended, Reena felt a deep sadness envelop her. She

stood there, trembling, as the weight of Vikram's words crashed over her like a tidal wave. "Why does he do this?" she whispered, her voice hoarse with grief.

Raman slumped onto the couch, his head in his hands. "I thought I could handle it, but I'm just so tired, Reena. I don't know how much more I can take."

In that moment, the reality of their situation settled heavily upon them both. The insults, the failures, the fear of losing everything

—it all coalesced into a singular point of despair.

"We can't stay here," Raman finally said, his voice barely above a whisper. "We need to make a change."

"What do you mean?" Reena asked, a flicker of hope igniting in her chest.

"I think it's time to sell the car and some jewelry," he said, a determined look in his eyes. "We could use the money to move in with your mother. It's not ideal, but it may give us a fresh start."

Reena's heart raced. The idea of moving back in with her parents was daunting, but the thought of facing Vikram's insults day in and day out felt unbearable. "You think they'll take us in?"

Raman nodded. "They may not have much in the way of resources, but at least we'll be out of here. We can regroup and figure out our next steps."

And just like that, as hope began to blossom amidst the shadows, Reena realized that the fight was far from over. She still had her family, and together they would face whatever came next. With a newfound sense of determination, she wiped her tears and looked at Raman.

"Let's do it. Let's make this change," she said, her heart swelling with a mix of fear and excitement.

As they began to make plans for their new journey, the weight of expectations felt slightly lighter, and for the first time in a long while, Reena felt a flicker of hope flickering in the darkness.

Chapter 4:
A New Dawn

The sun rose slowly over the horizon, casting a soft glow through the sheer curtains of Reena's childhood bedroom. She lay there, staring at the ceiling, surrounded by the relics of her past— posters of pop stars she had once idolized, books she had read and reread, and memories that felt both comforting and suffocating. The air felt heavy with the weight of her thoughts, and as she listened to the distant sound of her mother humming in the kitchen, a wave of nostalgia washed over her. But it was quickly replaced by the harsh reality of her current situation.

They had moved into her parents' home only days ago, having sold most of their belongings just to scrape together enough money to cover the essentials. The car, the jewelry, the little things that had once felt like symbols of stability, were now

distant memories. Reena had thought that returning home would bring her solace, but instead, it felt like a prison. Each day was punctuated by Vikram's taunts, which echoed in her mind like a haunting refrain, reminding her of her failures and inadequacies.

"Reena, are you awake?" her mother called from the kitchen, breaking the silence.

"Yes, Ma," Reena replied, forcing a smile as she rose from the bed. She padded into the kitchen, where the smell of freshly brewed chai filled the air. Her mother stood by the stove, stirring a pot of rice with a wooden spoon, her brow furrowed in concentration.

"Good morning, Aman!" her mother exclaimed, as her son bounded into the room, his energy a stark contrast to Reena's lethargy.

"Good morning, Dadi!" Aman chirped, rushing to hug his grandmother, his laughter filling the room with a warmth that momentarily chased away the shadows hanging over Reena's heart.

"Sit down, both of you. I made your favorite!" her mother said, placing a plate of aloo parathas on the table. Reena watched as Aman dug in with enthusiasm, his little hands grabbing at the food as if it was the most precious treasure in the world.

"See, Reena? It's not so bad here," her mother said, trying to lighten the mood. "We're all together, and that's what matters."

But Reena couldn't shake the feeling of defeat. Her mind was racing with thoughts of what Vikram would say next, how he would relish in her misfortune. She could almost hear his voice, dripping with condescension, reminding her of how she had let her life spiral out of control. "You did this to yourself," he would say. "Why don't you just give up?"

"Reena?" Her mother's voice cut through her thoughts. "Are you okay, dear?"

"Yeah, Ma. Just... thinking," Reena replied, forcing herself to smile. "I guess I'm still getting used to everything."

Her mother nodded, concern etched on her face. "It's a big change, I know. But we're here for you. Your father and I will help however we can."

Reena appreciated the sentiment, but the truth was that the weight of her situation was starting to feel unbearable. Raman had been searching for work in the city, but the job market was tough, and each rejection only added to the growing anxiety that loomed over their household. The more time they spent in her parents' home, the more she felt like a burden. It was a constant reminder of her brother's words, echoing in her mind, "You're a failure, and you always will be."

Later that afternoon, Reena found herself standing in front of the mirror, staring at her reflection. The woman looking back at her seemed foreign—her eyes were weary, her skin pale, and the

usual spark of hope that once shone brightly in her was dimmed by hopelessness. She silently willed herself to be strong, for Aman's sake if not her own. He deserved a mother who didn't crumble under the weight of despair.

"Reena, can we talk?" Raman's voice broke through her thoughts, and she turned to see him standing in the doorway, his expression serious yet tender.

"Of course," she replied, her heart racing as she stepped away from the mirror.

They moved to the small balcony that overlooked the garden, where the colors of blooming flowers were a stark contrast to the heaviness in her heart. The sun began to dip lower in the sky, casting a golden hue over everything, and for a brief moment, Reena felt a flicker of hope.

"Things have been rough," Raman started, his voice steady. "I've been thinking about our next steps."

Reena's stomach tightened at the thought of more changes. "What do you mean?"

"I believe we need to consider moving to a smaller city," he said, his eyes searching hers for understanding.

"Somewhere we can afford to live without the constant pressure of rent. I've heard there are opportunities there, and we could survive on our savings until I find work."

The words hit Reena like a cold splash of water. "But... what about here? What about my parents? I don't want to feel like I'm running away again," she said, her voice trembling.

"I know it seems drastic, but staying here is not helping us," Raman replied gently. "I can't stand seeing you like this, and I can't keep feeling like a failure because I'm unable to provide. If we move, we can start fresh. No more Vikram's taunts, no more living in the shadow of what we've lost."

Reena looked down at her hands, her mind racing with the implications of such a move. "But what if it doesn't work out, Raman? What if we're just trading one prison for another?"

"Then we try again. But if it's not going our way, Reena, then it's God's way," he said, his voice firm yet comforting. "We have to believe that something better is waiting for us. We just have to be brave enough to take the leap."

His words, though simple, ignited a flicker of optimism within her. Perhaps this was the change they needed. Perhaps moving would mean leaving behind the constant reminders of their failures and starting anew. With every passing moment, she felt a small part of her resolve to fight against the whispers of doubt that threatened to consume her.

"I want to believe that," she said softly, her heart beginning to swell with a sense of possibility. "But I'm scared, Raman."

"I am too," he admitted, taking her hands in his. "But we can face anything together, remember? We're a team. We just need to trust each other and take that first step."

For the first time in a long while, Reena looked into Raman's eyes and felt a glimmer of hope. Despite the chaos of their lives, they still had each other. They were still fighting, still dreaming. And maybe that was enough.

As the sun began to set, casting vibrant colors across the sky, Reena felt a sense of peace wash over her. The future was uncertain, but for the first time, she was willing to embrace it. She squeezed Raman's hands tightly, ready to take that leap of faith together.

"Let's do it," she said, her voice stronger now. "Let's move."

And as they stood together on that balcony, the weight of despair began to lift, replaced by the promise of a new dawn.

Chapter 5: Shadows of Doubt

The small town of Shantivan was a far cry from the bustling city where Reena had once lived. The air was fresher here, the trees lined the streets like sentinels, and the pace of life was slower.

When they first arrived, Reena had hoped that this change of scenery would also bring a change in fortune. They had rented a modest home on the outskirts, a simple two-bedroom house with a small garden that needed tending. Despite its imperfections, it felt like a new beginning.

Aman had settled into a nearby school, and though he missed the friends he'd left behind, he was excited about the prospect of making new ones. His laughter, like music, filled the home, a reminder that joy could still exist amidst the chaos. Yet, as weeks turned into months, the initial excitement of their new life began to wane, replaced by a heavy sense of uncertainty.

Raman had been tirelessly searching for work. Day after day, he scoured job listings, sent out applications, and networked. Each rejection felt like a dagger to

Reena's heart, piercing through the thin veil of hope that still clung to her. She wanted to support him, to be a pillar of strength in his time of struggle, but the burden of their situation began to weigh heavily on her, pulling her into the depths of despair.

As the sun dipped below the horizon, casting long shadows in their tiny kitchen, Reena stood by the sink, washing the few dishes they had left. The water felt cool against her hands, but the chill in her heart was far greater. She glanced up at the clock on the wall; it was almost dawn. She had been waking up early, hoping that the quiet hours before the world stirred would provide her with clarity, a chance to connect with God and seek guidance.

But each morning, as she sat cross-legged on the worn-out mat in the living room, her thoughts spiraled into darkness. She would close her eyes, take a deep breath, and try to focus, but the negative thoughts rushed in like a tide, drowning out her prayers. "Why did this happen to us?" she would think. "Where is God when we need help the most?" The questions felt like stones, heavy and unyielding, sinking into her soul.

It wasn't just the money that troubled her; it was the feeling of hopelessness that gnawed at her every waking moment. The days were long, and the nights were longer. She kept her worries to herself, not wanting to add to Raman's burdens. He was already so tied up in his search for a job, and every time she opened her mouth to speak, the words would die on her lips.

What could she say that would ease his struggle? Instead, she wore a mask of normalcy, feigning strength while her heart was in turmoil.

One particularly bleak morning, Reena woke before the sun had even begun to glow. She slipped out of bed, careful not to wake Raman or Aman, and made her way to the living room. The house was still, and the silence echoed in her ears. She settled onto the mat, attempting her morning ritual of prayer and meditation.

"Please, God, help us," she whispered into the stillness, her voice barely a murmur. "I don't know how much longer we can go on like this."

But as she searched for solace in her thoughts, the familiar shadows crept in. Doubt whispered insidiously, "What if there is no God? What if He has forgotten you?" Each question twisted like a knife, cutting deeper into her spirit.

Suddenly, tears blurred her vision. She felt utterly alone, trapped in her pain, with no way out. She couldn't share her struggles with Raman; he was already fighting his own battles. And Aman, with his innocent laughter and bright eyes, deserved a mother who could lift him up, not one who was crumbling under the weight of despair.

Days passed, and their situation grew increasingly dire. The little savings they had brought with them were dwindling, and the thought of how to put food on the table loomed like a dark cloud. Reena could see the worry etched on Raman's face, even when he tried to hide it. Each time he came home after another fruitless day, she felt a pang of guilt for not being able to contribute, for not being able to ease his burdens.

One evening, as they sat at the kitchen table, the smell of an empty pot simmering on the stove hung heavy in the air. Reena picked at the remnants of rice left from the previous meal, her stomach growling in protest. The silence was deafening, punctuated only by the occasional sound of Aman playing in his room.

"Raman," she said quietly, her voice trembling. "What are we going to do? We can't keep living like this."

He looked at her, his brow furrowed, the weight of their reality reflected in his eyes. "I'm trying, Reena. I really am," he replied. "But it feels like we're running out of options. I don't want to ask your parents for help, but I don't know how much longer we can go on without any income."

"Maybe we should consider going back..." she hesitated, the thought making her stomach churn. "To the city. We can ask Vikram for help until you find something stable."

Raman's expression darkened, and he shook his head vehemently. "No. I refuse to let him be our savior. We've come too far to turn back now."

"But what if it gets worse? We're already struggling to eat, Raman!" she burst out, frustration boiling over.

"Listen to me," he said, his voice steady but firm. "When there is a lot of darkness in the night, it means that the morning sunlight is about to come. Everything will be alright, but we won't ask Vikram or your mother for any help. We have to find a way to make this work."

Reena looked into his eyes, searching for the strength and determination that had once been so evident. "What if the morning never comes?" she whispered, her heart heavy with uncertainty.

Raman reached across the table, taking her hands in his. "It will come, Reena. We just have to believe in ourselves. We've faced so much already, and we're still standing. We can't give up now."

The warmth of his hands gave her a sliver of comfort, but the gnawing fear in her heart remained. She wanted to trust him, to believe that they would find a way through this darkness, but doubt hung around her like a shroud. The days turned into a blur of worry, and with each passing moment, the weight of their situation felt heavier, pressing down on her spirit.

As the sun set behind the horizon, painting the sky in hues of orange and purple, Reena found herself again in the living room, staring blankly at the wall. She longed for the peace that had once filled her heart, a solace she desperately sought but could not find.

But as she sat in that silence, she realized that she was not alone. She had Raman and Aman, and together they were a family, bound by love and resilience. The road ahead might be uncertain, but perhaps it was the journey itself that would lead them to the light they so desperately sought.

With that thought, she took a deep breath, willing herself to embrace whatever lay ahead. Together, they would face the shadows, and perhaps, just perhaps, they would find their way back into the light.

Chapter 6:
A Flicker of Hope

The days turned into weeks, and the weight of uncertainty continued to press down on Reena's heart like a suffocating blanket. Despite her efforts to remain hopeful, the shadows of despair clung to her, whispering doubts that reared their ugly heads at every quiet moment. She felt as though she was trapped in a cycle of negativity, where each thought spiraled deeper into despair. Raman's fruitless job search and the dwindling savings were constant reminders of their precarious situation.

Yet, amidst the turmoil, there was one bright spot: Aman. Their son's laughter was like a balm to her weary soul. He had an innate ability to find joy in the smallest of things, and his innocent outlook on life provided Reena with fleeting moments of reprieve from her worries. Each time she watched him play, her heart ached with both love and guilt. She wanted to give him the world, to shield him from the struggles that loomed over their family like a dark cloud.

One sun-drenched afternoon, Reena decided to take Aman to the local park. She thought that some fresh air and playtime would do them both good. As they arrived, the park was alive with the sounds of children's laughter, the rustling of leaves in the gentle breeze, and the distant chirping of birds. Reena felt a flicker of hope, a momentary escape from the suffocating weight of her thoughts.

Aman scampered off to join other children, his laughter ringing clear and bright. Reena settled onto a bench, allowing herself to watch him play. She felt an odd sense of peace, a reminder of the simple joys that life could offer. But just as the warmth of the sun began to soothe her, that familiar darkness crept back in.

It was then that she noticed a scruffy stray dog wandering through the park. Its fur was matted, and its ribs protruded sharply beneath its coat, a clear sign of neglect and hunger. The dog's eyes, however, were the most striking; they were filled with an innocent yearning, a desperate hope that tugged at Reena's heart. Against her better judgment, she felt compelled to act.

Reena reached into her bag, pulling out the few leftover biscuits she had brought for their outing. She broke one into pieces and extended her hand toward the dog, who cautiously approached, sniffing the air. As it took the biscuit from her hand, a surge of warmth flooded through her, surprising her with its intensity.

This simple act of kindness felt like a release, a moment of connection that transcended her worries.

"Hey there, little one," she said softly, her fingers brushing through the dog's fur as it devoured the biscuit. In that moment, she felt a sense of healing, as if the burden she had been carrying was lightened, if only for a fleeting second. She continued to feed the dog, each morsel exchanged between them bridging a gap of loneliness that had settled in her heart.

As days turned into weeks, feeding stray animals became a routine for Reena. Every visit to the park included a few biscuits, and soon, she found herself looking forward to those moments. The act of caring for the animals began to shift her perspective. With each dog she fed, with every hungry eye she met, she felt a flicker of connection to something greater, a sense of purpose that had eluded her for so long.

It was during one such day at the park that an idea sparked in her mind. While feeding a scruffy little dog with a lopsided ear, she recalled her grandmother's recipes, the ones that had filled their home with warmth and love. They had been family heirlooms, passed down through generations, bringing joy and comfort to those who savored them. What if she shared those recipes with the world?

With a newfound determination, Reena took the plunge and created a YouTube channel, dedicating it to her grandmother's cherished dishes. At first, she was hesitant, plagued by self-doubt. Who would want to watch her? But as she began to film, pouring her heart into each recipe, she felt a sense of liberation. Cooking became a form of therapy; the chopping, stirring, and seasoning were like a dance that freed her spirit.

To her astonishment, her videos began to gain traction. Viewers resonated with her warmth, her passion, and the nostalgic recipes that evoked memories of home-cooked meals. Before long, her channel blossomed into a vibrant community.

Comments poured in, filled with encouragement and gratitude, and for the first time in months, Reena felt a flicker of joy igniting within her.

And then, the unexpected happened. One of her videos went viral, catapulting her channel into the limelight. The financial struggles that had weighed heavily on her family began to lift. Brands reached out for collaborations, and ad revenue streamed in. What once felt impossible was now a reality; she was not only contributing to her family's income but also rekindling her love for cooking and connecting with others.

Raman, who had been searching for work diligently, found solace in Reena's newfound success.

Their home, once filled with tension and despair, began to breathe again. They laughed more, shared meals together, and even started dreaming of the future.

Reena could see the weight lifting from Raman's shoulders, a testament to their resilience as a family.

Even Vikram, who had once been a source of doubt in Reena's mind, expressed his shock and pride at her accomplishments. Their conversations shifted from worry to celebration, and their relationship, once strained, found new strength in mutual respect and support.

Yet, despite the positive changes, Reena still grappled with her negative thoughts. They lurked at the edges of her mind, whispering doubts that occasionally clouded her newfound happiness. But now, instead of succumbing to them, she recognized them as part of her journey. She understood that even in times of struggle, God was present, guiding her through the darkness.

It became clear to Reena that the stray dog she had met that day at the park had been more than just a hungry animal; it was a messenger of hope. The experience had opened her heart and reconnected her with her faith. She realized that God sees beyond the turmoil of the mind; He recognizes the purity of the heart.

As she continued to feed the stray dogs, Reena felt a sense of purpose that extended beyond her YouTube success. She organized food drives for local animal shelters, bringing her community together to care for those who had no voice. Each act of kindness, whether toward animals or fellow humans, reinforced the bond that connected them all.

Reena's journey had transformed her from a woman weighed down by negative thoughts to one who embraced the beauty of life, even amidst uncertainty. She learned that the path to healing is not linear; it is filled with ups and downs, moments of clarity, and times of confusion. But through it all, love, connection, and kindness remained the anchors that grounded her.

In time, she found peace not only in her actions but also within herself. The negative thoughts still visited, but they no longer held the same power over her. She had learned to acknowledge them without allowing them to dictate her emotions. Instead, she chose to focus on the love she had for her family, her passion for cooking, and the joy of giving back to her community.

www.ingramcontent.com/pod-product-compliance
Lightning Source LLC
LaVergne TN
LVHW092232080526
838199LV00104B/99